MW00438101

Don't Panic!

The Red Rovers (more often called the "Reject Rovers") were losing. There was nothing new about that, but now they were on the attack. It always made their forwards nervous, especially Kevin "Panic" Taylor.

By pure luck the ball had landed at his feet, and Kevin was just outside the penalty area with a clear run on goal.

The Crestmore Convenience Store Colts' goalie got to his feet hopefully and stretched.

He'd been sitting down, bored to death for the last hour, without a single shot to save.

He crouched, ready to fling himself at Kevin's shot – if it ever came.

"Steady. No need to panic. Keep calm," Kevin muttered to himself.

He could see the back of the net and imagined the way it would quiver when the ball went in. If only he could keep cool – just for once – and score a goal for the Rovers.

"Shoot, Kevin! Shoot!" Mr. Horowitz shouted from the sideline.

"Pass, Kevin!" Peter yelled.

Kevin looked up. He'd *love* to pass. Someone else could gladly have the job of shooting. As usual, however, Peter was hovering way out by the corner flag. He never came near the penalty area in case he got his uniform dirty. It was up to Kevin.

He could hear the Colts' defense pounding back to steal the ball. Any second now a leg would lunge out and scoop the ball away to safety. It was now or never.

Kevin glanced up at the goal to take aim.
That's when the familiar panic set in. The
goal seemed to shrink to the size of a flea,
and the goalie grew hands like shovels.

Kevin felt hot and dizzy. He was sweating.
When he swung his right leg forward, his toe
connected with the ground. Kevin fell flat on
his face. The ball rolled harmlessly into the
goalie's gloves.

"That's why they call you Thunderbolt,
Captain!" Peter called from the wing.

The Colts' goalie kicked the ball. It
bounced halfway up the field.

Stringbean, playing defense for the Reject
Rovers, jumped to head it, but too early. His

lanky body went down as the ball was going up. One of the Colts' strikers ran up to take control of it.

There was only the Rejects' goalie, Scuba, to beat. He stayed on his line. Scuba never came out in case someone went around him and made him look stupid. He preferred to look stupid in his goal. Instead, he always dived energetically – hence his nickname.

The Colts' striker shot and the ball soared toward the right top corner.

Scuba dived spectacularly for the bottom left corner. The ball bulged in the net.

The Colts' striker grinned and shook his head in disbelief. He shook hands with his teammates. There wasn't too much celebration. After all, it was his fifth goal that afternoon and the score was 11–0. The referee blew his whistle soon after.

"You have all the bad luck, Panic," he said, shaking his head at Kevin. "Someone has to lose, but your team makes it look easy."

"Yeah," Kevin agreed, "we've had a lot of practice."

They trudged off the field miserably.

"Why didn't you score? You had an open goal!" Scuba moaned to Kevin.

"The ball wobbled – it was a hopeless shot," Kevin scowled.

"Not as hopeless as you are. What use is a captain who panics every single time he sees the goal?"

"What use is a goalie who always dives the wrong way?" Kevin snapped back. "We'd do better with a stuffed dummy in goal. At least it would keep still."

"Now, there's no point in you two arguing," said Mr. Horowitz, Scuba's dad. "You were just unlucky, that's all. The slope was against you in the second half."

Kevin caught Scuba's eye and almost grinned. They knew Mr. Horowitz had been reading his newspaper for most of the game.

He always said that. Whether the score was 5–0 or 22–0, the Reject Rovers were always unlucky, according to Mr. Horowitz.

He was the coach only because the Rovers had to use his construction van to get to their games. It was a good thing they had red uniforms; they didn't show the brick dust.

"You rejects didn't lose *again*, did you?" a mocking voice called from behind them.

Kevin turned his head to see Sean Slacker. Slacker played for the Dixon Deli Dynamos, who had been playing on the next field.

The Dynamos were first in the District Junior League, which Slacker liked to remind Kevin at every possible chance. He was the last person Kevin wanted to talk to right now.

"Don't you want to be with your own team?" Kevin asked.

"Of course," Slacker said, "but first I wanted to see how you did – because I care."

"I suppose you won again?" Scuba said, avoiding Slacker's gaze.

"Four to one," Slacker said. "I even scored a hat trick. It could have been more, but I'm saving myself for our next game."

"Why? Who are you playing?"

Even as he asked the question Kevin could guess the answer.

"Don't you know? We're playing *you* in two weeks. It's going to be a massacre. I've told the ref to bring his calculator to keep the score."

Kevin held back a groan. Scuba closed his eyes. He was imagining himself picking the ball out of the net every ten seconds for the entire game.

"Anyway," Slacker said, as neither of them spoke, "you haven't answered my question."

"What question?" Kevin said. He was walking fast to get away from Slacker.

Slacker kept up with him. "Today. Did you lose? Again?"

"Yes."

"What was the score?"

"Eleven–zero," Kevin said sarcastically. "It could have been more, but we're saving ourselves for our next game."

They'd reached the pavilion. With relief, Kevin and Scuba went inside.

Slacker followed them into the locker room. He hadn't finished rubbing it in.

"So tell me again. How many games is it that you've lost in a row?"

"Get lost, Slacker! We're getting changed!" Kevin growled.

"Come on, how many have you lost? Just tell me, then I'll go. Have you won any games this season?"

"No!"

"Tied any?"

"No!"

"So you've lost *every single* game?"

"I just said so. Now get out!"

"You lost them all last season, didn't you? How many games is that altogether?"

"Why does it matter? What do you care?"

"I just want to know."

"Thirty-nine games, okay?"

Sean Slacker whistled. "Thirty-nine defeats in a row. Is that some sort of record? You might just be the worst team in the world."

"Get lost, Slackjaw!"

Slacker retreated out of the doorway in a hail of soccer cleats and shin guards.

He made his way back to where the Dynamos' locker room was, grinning to himself and shaking his head. "Thirty-nine games in a row. Maybe that *is* a record. I think I'll have to look it up."

13

2

____

On the Record

Sean Slacker found his dad's *Guinness Book of World Records* on the bottom shelf of the bookcase. He wiped the dusty cover with his sleeve. He hadn't looked at it in a long time.

He read about the world's longest beard (over fifteen feet), the world's biggest hamburger (two and a half tons), and the world's busiest dentist (he'd pulled out two million teeth).

At last he found the sports section near the back. There was the list of great winning teams around the world. Sean, however, wasn't reading about the winners this time.

He was looking for the most hopeless team in soccer history. There, at the bottom of page 124, he found them.

"The worst run of defeats was recorded by the Doddering Ducks. In the 1951–2 and 1952–3 seasons they lost thirty-nine games in a row. Their terrible run finally came to an end with a 0–0 tie against the Hardly Athletic team."

Thirty-nine games. Sean stroked his pointed nose thoughtfully.

So the Reject Rovers weren't the worst team in history – yet. Unfortunately, somebody had beat them to that too.

Then he smiled. The Rovers had *also* lost thirty-nine games in a row. So they were only one game away from breaking the record. That one game was against Sean's own team, the Dixon Deli Dynamos. A thin smile spread across Sean's weasel face.

In two more weeks he would help the
Reject Rovers enter history as *the worst team
of all time*. They'd never live it down. He
could just see Kevin Taylor's face when he
heard. Sean decided he would make sure the
news got around.

He hadn't forgotten what had happened
three years ago. Kevin Taylor had just started
the Rovers when Sean had generously offered
to be their captain. The team had voted and
they'd actually turned him down. Him! Sean
Slacker – with more talent in his big toe than
their whole team put together.

The insult of being rejected by a bunch of rejects still made him boil with anger. Ever since, he'd been waiting to get even. Now the perfect chance had fallen into his lap.

As he put the book back on the shelf Sean's eyes fell on the local paper. It was open at the sports page.

There was the usual roundup of the local junior league by someone named Steve Ryan.

It gave Sean an idea, an idea so brilliant he had to go out to the hall mirror and blow himself a big kiss. The Reject Rovers were about to become famous!

17

Kevin Taylor had no idea that fame was about to call on him. At that moment he was more worried about his poster collection.

"Kevin, you can hang them up in the spare bedroom," his mom told him for the third time.

"I don't want to put them up there," Kevin protested. "I want them here. In *my* room. I have them just the way I want them."

"What's the difference? You're just being annoying about this," his mom said.

18

Kevin flopped down on his bed. He knew he was being annoying, but he had a right to be. This was his bedroom. It had always been his bedroom. Now his mom wanted to give it to a renter and make him move down the hall into the spare room.

"Why can't *he* go in the spare room? I live here. I was here first."

"I've told you, the spare room's too small," Kevin's mom said. "Also, I want him to have a little privacy. In this room he'll be able to get away from you and your sister arguing all the time."

"We don't argue all the time!" Kevin argued. "We only argue when she's wrong."

His sister Fiona was thirteen, an age when there ought to be a ban on sisters, in Kevin's opinion.

With alarm, Kevin saw his mom starting to peel one of his posters off the wall.

"Don't do that!" Kevin yelled. "You'll tear them or wrinkle them or something." His soccer posters were his pride and joy.

They started with his favorite, the U.S. Olympic team, over his bed. The teams then ran along the wall to his tenth favorite, the Raleigh Rovers (same initials as the Rejects) over the radiator.

Gloomily, Kevin started to take them down while his mom cleared out his closet.

"Anyway, I still don't see why we need to take in a renter," Kevin muttered.

"I've told you. We need the extra money now that I'm only working part-time."

"What if I don't like him?" Kevin said.

"He sounds like a perfectly nice young man. His name's Alex. He's a student teacher at Grimley High."

"A teacher?" Kevin groaned. "You didn't say he was a teacher!"

"Didn't I? What's wrong with that?"

"He'll talk about tadpoles and magnets. He'll want us to line up for breakfast! I'll have to raise my hand to go to the bathroom."

"Don't be silly, Kevin. You'll like him."

"Oh yeah? What's his favorite soccer team?"

"How would I know?" his mom said, exasperated. "He may not even like soccer. There are people in this universe, Kevin, believe it or not, who manage to live their lives without soccer."

"Only boring ones," Kevin said. "Didn't you ask him any questions? He could be a cat burglar. He could be planning to steal everything we own while we sleep."

"As long as he cleans up afterward," Kevin's mom said absently.

Kevin took down his last team poster (the state university team that had played an exhibition last year) and looked around. His room didn't look like his room anymore.

He was sure he was not going to like Alex. He had enough of teachers at school.

His thoughts were suddenly interrupted by the phone ringing. Thumping downstairs, Kevin picked up the receiver. A voice said, "Hello, does Mr. Taylor live there?"

"You probably want my mom. She's upstairs," Kevin said.

"No, I don't. I actually want to speak to a Mr. Kevin Taylor."

Kevin hesitated. He tried to think what he'd done wrong lately. What trouble could he be in? It didn't sound like his teacher, Mr. Rees, whose voice could shatter windows. This voice sounded smooth and friendly.

"That's me. I'm Kevin Taylor," he answered at last.

"Oh! I just thought you sounded kind of young. I was told you manage a soccer team called the Rocket Rovers."

"The Reject Rovers – I mean Red Rovers," Kevin corrected. "I'm the player-manager, and the captain too."

"Great. Well my name's Steve Ryan. I'm a sports reporter with *The Grimley Gazette*. I was wondering if we could come and do a story on your team."

Kevin was stunned. Speechless.

"Hello? Are you still there?" Ryan asked.

"Yes... yes... yes, of course I am," Kevin stammered.

"You mean 'yes' we can do the story?"

"Yes," Kevin said. He sounded like an answering-machine message.

"Wonderful! I'd like to get the whole team together. Take some photos. Are you practicing or anything this evening?"

"Oh, yes," Kevin lied, "we practice almost every evening over at Riverside Park."

"Okay. I'll meet you there in an hour, if that's okay with your mom," Mr. Ryan said.

Kevin put down the phone in shock. How had *The Grimley Gazette* found out about the Reject Rovers? Why on earth were they interested in a team as hopeless as his? Kevin couldn't figure it out.

Picking up the phone again he punched in Scuba's number. Wait until the rest of the team heard about this. They were going to get their pictures in the paper – just like the pros!

3

Facing the Press

All the Rovers were at the park by the time Kevin got there. In fact, most of them had been waiting half an hour.

"Where's the reporter?" Scuba asked anxiously.

"He said he'd meet us here. What are those for?" Kevin pointed to Scuba's sunglasses.

"I thought they'd look cool. You know, for the pictures."

"You're supposed to be our goalie – not a movie star," Kevin grumbled. He sniffed the air. "What's that awful smell? It stinks just like a wet dog."

"It's Peter. He's wearing his dad's aftershave," Scuba said with a laugh.

Kevin was about to make a speech about acting like a serious soccer team when a red car pulled up. Steve Ryan got out, along with the photographer from *The Grimley Gazette*.

Ryan turned out to be a freckled young man in a brown suit that was way too big for him. He strode toward them briskly with his hand outstretched.

"Steve Ryan. *Grimley Gazette*. Which one of you is Kevin?"

"I am," Kevin said, stepping forward to shake his hand. He felt important talking to a real reporter.

"Great, Kev. This is Ted. He's going to be taking the photos."

Ted winked and showed everyone the large camera he was carrying.

"Are you guys ready?" he said. They all nodded eagerly.

"Do you want to take the photos now?" Scuba asked, adjusting his sunglasses. "I could go in the goal and dive around."

Ryan shook his head. "We'll do that later. First I'd like to ask Kev a few questions about the team. Shall we sit down somewhere?"

Kevin followed Ryan over to a park bench. The rest of the Rovers went too. They had never seen a reporter, and they were anxious not to miss anything.

It ended up with twelve of them squashed on one bench.

It took several minutes for Kevin to get them to settle down and listen. At last they were ready to start the interview.

"Now," Steve Ryan said, getting out his notebook. "The Reject Rovers. That's a pretty unusual name for a soccer team. Why did you choose it?"

"It was kind of a joke to start with," Kevin explained. "None of us had a team to play for so Scuba, Stringbean, and I, we thought..."

"Scuba and Stringbean?" Ryan's pencil had stopped scribbling.

"Yeah, they're nicknames. We've all got them. It's sort of a team rule." He pointed out the members of the team. "Dancing Pete, VJ, Dangerous, Baby Joe..."

"Baby Joe?"

"It's because he can't stop dribbling... Would you like to write all of these down?" Kevin asked.

"Uh, maybe later. You were saying how you got the name Rejects..."

"Oh yeah. Scuba, Stringbean, and I decided to start our own team. We officially called ourselves the Red Rovers, but Reject Rovers became our team nickname because... well, no other teams wanted us."

"That's because we stink," Stringbean added helpfully. Kevin glared at him.

"How long exactly have the Rovers been together?" Mr. Ryan asked.

"This is our third season. We're still improving. The best is yet to come," Kevin said. He'd heard a manager say that once on TV and thought it sounded good.

"But what about results, Kev? The Rovers haven't won too many games this season, have they?"

"We've had bad luck," Kevin admitted.

"Rotten referees," Scuba said.

"It doesn't help that Kevin keeps missing the goal!" Stringbean added.

Kevin shot him another withering look. He was hoping Steve Ryan didn't want to ask too many questions about the Rovers' dismal record. Unfortunately, those were exactly the kind of details he seemed interested in.

Kevin knew the statistics for this season by heart. *Played 19, Won 0, Tied 0, Lost 19. Goals for: 3, Goals against: 104.*

"So if you lost all twenty games last season and nineteen this season, that means you've lost thirty-nine games in a row, Kev. That's right isn't it, thirty-nine?" Mr. Ryan said.

Kevin had to admit it was, though he wished Mr. Ryan would stop repeating it.

"You don't have to put that in the story, do you?" he asked. "We don't want people to think... well... we're the worst team ever."

"No, no, of course not!" Mr. Ryan rubbed his chin. "This is just background stuff, Kev. Reporters have to check out all these little facts, you know."

After that Ted wanted to take some pictures. He suggested they just do their normal practice session while he snapped a few shots.

The Rovers looked blankly at their manager. *Practice sessions?* They never had real practice sessions...

Kevin thought quickly. "Line up," he said. "We'll start with penalty-shot practice."

There was a lot of pushing and shoving to be at the front of the line. Everyone wanted their picture in the paper.

Stringbean got there first. He played for a junior basketball team and was a head taller than the rest.

He stood halfway down the field and charged at the ball like an express train.

His shot sailed into orbit about thirty yards over the goal. Even Scuba didn't bother to dive – and he dove at *everything*.

Ted's camera clicked. "Nice try," he said and gave them another wink.

Dancing Pete was next. No one had ever actually asked him to shoot before. He took a few steps forward and scuffed the ball gently along the ground. It didn't even come close to the goal.

Then it was Kevin's turn. He was beginning to wonder if taking pictures was such a good idea after all. Now it was up to him, as the official player-manager, to show that the Rovers were not a joke team.

He placed the ball carefully on the spot. Ted moved in a step closer to get a good shot of him. Scuba crouched low, ready to dive. Kevin began to run up. At the last instant he looked up at the goal. That was his big mistake. Panic took over. What if he missed? What if he made an idiot of himself?

Gripped by fear, he completely forgot to look down at the ball. His foot swung wildly and he spun around like a top. When he looked again the ball was exactly where it had been before.

"Did you get that one, Ted?" Steve Ryan said as he tried to keep a straight face.

Ted winked back. "Great stuff," he said. "Now just a few of the goalie. Why don't you give him a few shots, Steve?"

Steve Ryan lined up his first shot. Scuba could hardly see the ball through his dark sunglasses.

The first shot hit him on the nose and sent the glasses spinning into the air.

The second shot hit the post, cannoned off the back of his head with a loud *thonk*, and then sailed into the net.

Scuba missed seven out of seven. Ted took lots of pictures.

Last of all, they lined up for a team photo. Ted organized them in two rows, arms folded, just like the teams in Kevin's posters.

"Well thanks a lot, guys," Steve Ryan said. "I think we got what we wanted."

"Will we be in the paper tomorrow?" Kevin asked.

"We'll do our best to make the deadline. Anyway, good luck in your next game. I think you'll need it."

"Yeah, we don't stand a chance," Kevin said. "Not against the Dixon Deli Dynamos. They're first in the league."

"I've heard Sean's a talented striker."

"Sean Slacker?" Kevin asked, confused.

"That's him. I hear he's had twenty-one goals this season," Mr. Ryan said.

"Who told you that?"

"Oh, one of you must have mentioned it. Ready to head out, Ted?"

Mr. Ryan and Ted thanked them and said good-bye.

Kevin thought about it later. He couldn't remember anyone talking about Sean Slacker.

4
—————

The Fame Game

Kevin had told everyone at school that the Rovers were going to be in *The Grimley Gazette*. He hadn't meant to, he just couldn't help it. Miles Elliot had been showing off in the playground.

Miles was one of Sean Slacker's friends. He played for the Dixon Deli Dynamos, and Kevin couldn't stand him. Miles bragged that his uncle had been on the radio talking about bird-watching or something.

Kevin had waited until Miles had finished boasting. Then he'd dropped his bombshell.

"As a matter of fact, I was just talking to Steve Ryan last night."

"Who is Steve Ryan?" Miles asked, rolling his eyes.

"Don't you know who Steve Ryan is, Miles? I thought you knew something about soccer. Steve Ryan writes the sports page for *The Grimley Gazette*. He called me last night to talk about my team."

Kevin could tell no one believed him. Luckily Scuba was there to back him up. Soon they were telling the whole story. By lunch it was all around the school.

Kevin Taylor had been interviewed for the paper. The Reject Rovers were going to be in *The Grimley Gazette*. There would be pictures. Kevin had been driven home in a silver Rolls Royce. (Okay, so he'd gotten a little carried away with the story.)

As the day went on, Kevin's fame grew and grew. He noticed younger kids at school whispering and pointing. When he was lining up for lunch, a first grader tugged at his sleeve. The small boy pushed a pencil and a piece of paper at Kevin.

"What's this for?"

"Autograph," the boy said.

"What?"

"Aren't you the guy that's gonna be in the newspaper?"

"Yeah, that's me."

"Well, can I have your autograph? I collect them," the little kid said.

Kevin had signed his name, laughing, but it felt good. At last he was somebody at school. Everyone knew his name. He began to imagine what his photo would look like in the paper.

"Kevin Taylor, manager." Or *"Kevin Taylor, player-manager of the Rovers."* Better still, *"Kevin Taylor, the Rovers' top striker."*

* * *

Sean Slacker was the first to get ahold of *The Grimley Gazette.* He'd run all the way to the convenience store after school. Kevin was coming out of the school doors. A crowd of admirers was with him.

"Have you seen it?" Slacker said, running up out of breath.

"Seen what?" Kevin drawled.

"The paper." He waved his copy under Kevin's face.

"Is it in there?" Kevin asked eagerly.

"Oh, yes, it's in there all right. A big story. All over the back page."

Kevin grabbed the paper. He wondered why Slacker was looking so happy. Turning to the back page, he found out. The headline was in big bold letters over a team photo of the Rovers: "Is This The Worst Team in History?" The article by Steve Ryan said:

"Next week, a local boys' team, the Reject Rovers, will make soccer history. If they lose the game they'll have lost forty games in a row. Forty! That's a record. According to the Guinness Book of World Records *it will earn them the title of 'The Worst Team of All Time.' No wonder they call themselves the Rejects! I went to see them practice, and I soon found out what makes the Rovers such a bunch of losers…"*

Kevin looked at the photos below. There was the ball bouncing off Scuba's nose...

There was Stringbean watching his shot enter a distant galaxy, and him – Kevin "Panic" Taylor – kicking thin air. "*Whoops! Missed again, Kevin!*" the caption said.

Kevin lowered the paper in horror, unable to read on. Why hadn't anyone told him?

They'd been tricked. The story made them sound like a joke. They were about to become famous as *The Worst Team in History*. No wonder Steve Ryan had wanted to meet them!

Kevin's mind raced ahead. What would the rest of the team say when they saw this? They were sure to blame him – their manager. After all, he'd brought Mr. Ryan to see them. What about the others? His friends, his classmates, everyone at school?

By tomorrow morning nearly everyone would have seen the paper. They were bound to. He'd told them all to buy a copy.

Miles Elliot grabbed the paper from his hand. The others crowded around to see.

"There's Kevin!"

"Look at his face! What a moron!"

"He can't even kick the ball!"

"Awesome, isn't it?" said Sean Slacker. "I mean, I think people should know just how awful you guys are. The worst team in history. You could put it on your uniforms."

Kevin saw the look of cruel triumph on Slacker's face. Suddenly he understood.

"It was you, wasn't it?" he said. He got right into Slacker's face. "You set all this up. You called the paper. You told Steve Ryan all about us."

Slacker tried to push him away. He backed up a few steps.

"Don't be stupid! Do you think I'd go to all that trouble? Just for your pathetic team?"

"So how come he knew about you?"

"Who did?"

"Steve Ryan. He knew your name."

"So what?"

"He even knew how many goals you'd scored this season. Twenty-one."

Slacker's eyes betrayed his mistake.

"You're nuts. He could have easily found that out himself."

"Why should he? You couldn't help showing off, could you, Slackjaw?"

Sean Slacker looked around for support. The crowd around them had closed in. They sensed a fight, but Slacker didn't want that. He wanted Kevin to look stupid.

"At least I've got something to show off about," he taunted. "Not like the worst team in history."

"We're not. Not yet."

"You will be, when we thrash you."

"*If* you thrash us," Kevin said rashly.

"Oh yeah! You think we won't? You losers are so slow a team of snails could beat you!"

That was when Kevin made his big mistake. That was when he should have turned around and walked away.

He should have said something intelligent like, "I'd rather play snails than a slug like you." That's not what he said, though.

With everyone watching, he narrowed his eyes at Sean Slacker and held out his hand.

"Want to bet?" he demanded.

"What? A bet on who'll win on Saturday?" Slacker said.

"Yeah. If you're so sure."

"You're on." Slacker took his hand. "The loser has to clean the other player's cleats..."

"All right," Kevin agreed.

"... by licking the mud off," Slacker added.

"You must be joking! I'm not licking your stupid cleats!"

"Too late," Slacker said. "We just shook on the bet." He turned to the others. "You all saw that, didn't you?"

The others nodded in agreement. Kevin was shaking hands when Slacker had spoken. There was no way out. The bet was made.

The crowd around him was grinning. They couldn't wait to see him eat dirt.

44

"Anyway, you haven't won yet. We'll see on game day," Kevin said weakly. He walked away by himself. The others stayed behind with Sean Slacker.

As he crossed to the other side of the street Slacker's voice reached him. "Hey, Taylor! I almost forgot – will you give us your autograph?"

5

Remove the Renter

Kevin kicked a stone into the gutter. What had he done? He'd just bet that the Reject Rovers would win on Saturday. He might as well have bet that he'd be the first man on Mars. It was impossible. Hopeless.

They'd be lucky if they kept the Dynamos' score down to less than ten. As far as Kevin could see his whole life would be ruined. The Rovers would forever be known as the worst team in history – the team that had lost a record forty games in a row.

They'd have to split up. Who would want to play for them? They'd be a joke.

You'd only have to mention the name, Reject Rovers, and everyone would fall down laughing.

All that was bad enough. It had taken a genius to make it worse. The bet with Slacker was the most stupid thing that Kevin had ever done.

He could picture the moment after the match. The Dixon Deli Dynamos would be slapping each other on the back. The Rovers would be trailing off the field, heads down. Then Slacker would step forward with a big smirk on his face. There, in front of everyone, he would remind Kevin of their bet.

He'd hand over his muddy cleats, saying, "Lick them clean, Taylor. Come on!"

Kevin wondered if he could move to the North Pole before next week. Maybe it was too cold for soccer there.

He opened the back door and drooped into the kitchen. Someone was sitting at the table having coffee with his mom. Kevin didn't even glance at them.

"Oh, here's Kevin. How was school?" his mom asked.

"Don't ask," Kevin said.

"That bad? Never mind, I've got someone I'd like you to meet. This is our new renter, Alex Hernandez."

Kevin had completely forgotten that the renter was moving in today. That was all he needed.

He turned to meet the person sitting with his mom.

It was a girl, older than Kevin's sister but not as old as his mom.

She had dark curly hair. It was held back with a red headband, but lots of it seemed to be escaping. The girl held out her hand to Kevin, beaming at him.

"Hi, Kevin. I'm Alex."

Kevin opened and shut his mouth like a goldfish. "You're... you're... not a man."

"I know. Sorry about that. It's the name Alex. I should have said in my letter that Alex is short for Alexandria. People often expect me to be a man."

Kevin's mom nodded. "I even had a shaving mirror put in the bathroom." They both went into fits of giggles.

"Great," Kevin said. "Just great. Well that makes it a perfect day."

He dumped his bag on the floor and stomped upstairs to his bedroom.

Kevin's mom sighed. "Sorry about that. He can be so rude sometimes. Don't worry, though – he'll be much better once he gets to know you."

❀ ❀ ❀

Kevin lay on his bed, staring at the ceiling. It was absolutely the last straw. He'd just had the worst day of his life at school, he'd made a stupid bet, and now the renter turned out to be a girl. With his mom and his sister, that meant he'd be outnumbered three-to-one in the house.

His sister was bound to think Alex was great. She'd probably borrow her clothes and start to talk like her.

When Kevin wanted to watch soccer on TV, Alex and his sister would outvote him for the remote control – probably for some mushy love story.

It wasn't fair. He didn't want a renter in the first place. He certainly didn't want one who was a teacher *and* a woman.

Why should he have to give up his bedroom to Alex?

That was it. Why should he? He'd get rid of her. He'd think of a plan to make sure she *didn't* stay in the house. The idea almost made him forget about the upcoming game.

By the time his mom called him for supper, Kevin had put stage one of his plan into operation. He'd called Scuba and asked him to come over later.

Kevin said little at dinner. When Alex tried to ask friendly questions, he gave her short answers. He went to Grimley Park Elementary. It was an okay school. Yes, he liked soccer.

"Kevin is the manager of his own soccer team, aren't you, Kevin?" his mom said encouragingly.

"Yeah," Kevin said, "but you wouldn't be interested. We're bad. Really awful."

"I doubt that. Maybe I could come and watch you sometime," Alex suggested.

Kevin gave her a dark look. He had enough trouble without her poking her nose into his business. She probably had never seen a soccer game in her entire life.

When Scuba arrived, Kevin smuggled him quickly upstairs to his bedroom.

"Do you have them?"

"Yeah," Scuba said. "They're in here, but you still haven't said what it's all about."

"Let's see them," Kevin said.

Scuba put the shoebox down on the bed. The lid had a row of air holes in it. Inside were his two pet mice, Salt and Pepper. They climbed over each other and sniffed the air.

"It's too bad they're not bigger or scarier or something," Kevin said.

"Why?"

"I wish they were rats," Kevin whispered. "She'll hate them. We're going to put them in her bed and wait for the screams."

"In your sister's bed?"

"No, dumbo! I told you on the phone. It's this student teacher, Alex. She's the new renter. If she thinks we have rats in the house, she'll leave. She'll be out of here like a shot."

Scuba stroked Pepper's soft fur. He looked doubtful.

"It'll work, you'll see. I'll be able to have my old room back," Kevin said.

"They're not rats, Kevin, they're mice," Scuba objected. "Anyway, what if this Alex person frightens them?"

"She won't. She'll take one look and run out of the house. Grown-ups are like that about rats. They only have to see one and they completely lose it."

They climbed the stairs quietly to Alex's room. Scuba had Salt and Pepper hidden under his sweater, but no one saw them.

Alex was still downstairs helping Kevin's mom wash the dinner dishes. Scuba hid the mice under her comforter. They were bound to come out and explore sooner or later.

Ten minutes later they heard Alex coming upstairs. They watched her from Kevin's bedroom, hiding behind the door.

Alex went into her room and closed her door. Kevin gave a thumbs-up sign to Scuba. They waited for the screams.

Five minutes passed. Ten. Twenty. After half an hour, Scuba started to worry. Not a sound was coming from upstairs. What if the renter had accidentally sat on Salt or Pepper? What if she'd attacked them with a shoe?

"Maybe she hasn't seen them yet," Kevin said. "We better go check."

"How?" Scuba said. "We can't exactly walk in and say, 'Excuse me, have you seen the mice we hid in here to scare you?'"

"We'll say we saw a rat. Then we can find them while she's on a chair, hollering."

They crept upstairs and listened at the door. There was still no sound. Kevin knocked on the door and flung it open.

"RATS!" he shrieked. "We just saw a big ugly rat come in here!"

Kevin stopped. Both of them stared.

Alex was sitting on her bed with Pepper on her shoulder. Salt was playing happily in her lap.

"It's okay. They're only mice," she laughed. "Aren't they great? Do they belong to you?"

Scuba was so relieved that his pets were safe, he completely forgot that Alex was supposed to be the enemy. Soon he was sitting on the bed, telling her all about his pets.

In the meantime, Kevin was staring in amazement at his old room. Alex had already made a lot of changes. A guitar was propped in the corner. The walls were covered in posters of faraway places. Kevin's eye took in the Brazilian soccer player with the ball at his feet.

Alex's blue jogging suit was draped over a chair. There was a badge on the top pocket.

"What's this?" Kevin asked.

Alex stopped playing with the mice and smiled at him.

"Oh, I'm very proud of that. It's my coaching badge."

"What do you coach?"

"Soccer. I did it as part of my teacher training. It was great!"

Scuba and Kevin looked at each other.

"I've always wanted to coach a soccer team. It's too bad they won't let me near the school team where I'm teaching."

"You could coach us," Scuba said.

"No she couldn't," Kevin said quickly. "We've already got a manager. Me."

"You don't know how to coach. We don't even have normal practice sessions."

"I'm the manager," Kevin insisted, "and we don't need any help."

"Oh, no, of course we don't!" Scuba said. "That's why we're last in the league. That's why we're going to get thrashed on Saturday. That's why we're going to be the worst team of all time."

"I saw today's paper," Alex admitted. "Will you really be breaking this record?"

Kevin nodded. "Looks like it."

"Unless we get a lot better," said Scuba. "Alex could help us, Kevin."

"It's too late," Kevin said. "We've got less than two weeks before the game."

Alex shrugged. "It's your team. If you want
I could watch you practice after school
tomorrow. It's up to you, though. You're the
manager."

"Kevin?" Scuba said.

Kevin scowled. "I'll think about it," he said.

6

Countdown to Disaster

The next day at school started badly for
Kevin. When he walked into the classroom
he had the feeling that everyone was waiting
for him. He sat down in his seat. Something
was taped to the table.

It was his picture, the one from *The
Grimley Gazette* that showed him missing the
ball completely. *"Whoops! Missed again,
Kevin!"* the caption reminded him.

Kevin flushed red. He could hear giggles all
around the classroom.

He swung around furiously and saw Sean Slacker and Miles Elliot doubled up with laughter.

"You think this is funny?" Kevin said to Slacker, ripping up the picture.

"Not as funny as your face right now," Slacker hooted.

"Give us your autograph, Kevin!" Miles jeered loudly.

"Oooh, Kevin! You're so famous!" sang Amanda Ross, pretending to faint.

Kevin sat back down. He got out his book and buried his face in it. He didn't want anyone to see how red his face was. It wasn't fair. He'd get Sean Slacker for this. He'd show him somehow.

Unfortunately, that was only the beginning. Slacker had been busy.

Everywhere he went, Kevin found the *Gazette* pictures on display. There was one taped on his locker in the hallway. There was one on the mirror in the boys' rest room.

When their teacher, Mr. Rees, pulled down the movie screen, there was the team photo of the Reject Rovers with the headline, *"Is This The Worst Team in History?"*

Mr. Rees asked Kevin if he had put it there. He couldn't understand why the whole class burst out laughing.

Worst of all was lunchtime. In the lunch line, everyone was snickering at Kevin. It wasn't until he sat down that he discovered the piece of paper stuck to his back. In black felt pen someone had scrawled:

As soon as he got home Kevin ran upstairs. He slammed his door and buried his face in his pillow. If this was what life was going to be like he didn't want to go to school. He'd have to stay in his room forever. Later there was a knock on his bedroom door.

"Go away!"

"Kevin? It's me, Alex."

"Go away!"

Alex poked her head around the door. "I came to ask you about practice tonight. Do you want me to come... or not?"

Kevin looked up from his pillow. He'd forgotten Alex's offer. He hadn't even talked to any of Rovers about having a practice.

"What's the use?" he said. "We're losers. We are the worst team in history. I'm the worst manager. Just ask anyone. Slacker told everyone, and now they're all coming to watch us lose the game. It sounds like the social event of the season," he added bitterly.

Alex came in and sat down at his desk. "So who's this Slacker character?"

Kevin told her. He told her all about Sean Slacker and *The Grimley Gazette*. About the pictures that had appeared all around school. He even told her about his stupid bet.

Alex listened. She was a good listener. She didn't interrupt like most people did. At the end she said, "So, there's only one way out."

"What?" Kevin said hopelessly. He didn't see any way out.

"You just have to win the game. Then you won't be the worst team of all time, you'll be heroes. Even better, Sean Slacker will lose the bet. He'll be the one to look stupid instead of you."

Kevin hadn't really thought of it like that. Alex was right. There was, however, one big problem. "You haven't seen us play," he said. "We'll never beat Slacker's team in a million years. That reporter was right – we're hopeless."

"Let me be the judge of that," Alex said. "Come on, get your cleats. Call the others and tell them to get over to the field."

An hour later, the Rovers were gathered
at Riverside Park. Alex came in her jogging
suit. She let Kevin introduce her to the rest of
the team.

They started with a simple scrimmage
game, so that Alex could watch them play.

Kevin kicked off. He passed the ball to
Baby Joe. Baby Joe went on a long dribble
that took him past five players and back to
where he started. Dancing Pete stood out on
the wing, shouting, "Pass! Pass!" When the
ball eventually came to him, he passed to
Stringbean. It would have been a good pass
if Stringbean had been on the same side.
Stringbean did what he always did – hoofed
the ball with all his might up the other end.

64

"Mine! Leave it!" Scuba shouted, coming out to catch the ball.

He collided with Dangerous, who always went for anything that moved. The ball bounced once and nestled in the net.

"Goal!" Stringbean shouted. "At least we scored one."

They all looked at Alex. Her mouth was still open. Kevin hadn't been exaggerating when he'd said they were bad.

"Well, there's plenty to work on," she said. Soon Alex had them dribbling in and out of rows of cones she'd brought along. They passed the ball in triangles with one touch. (Most of them had never received a pass from one of their own players.)

Scuba practiced diving in the goal. He discovered that when he kept his eyes open, he sometimes went the right way and saved a shot. They practiced corners, with Peter making the change in direction. The tenth time Peter got the ball off the ground.

Kevin and Scuba jumped for it together.

The ball glanced off Kevin's head before he had time to panic. It hit the inside of the post and rebounded into the net.

"Goal!" Kevin said, astonished. "I scored a goal... didn't I?"

"A peach," Alex said. "That was a beautiful header from Pete's perfect cross."

Dancing Pete glowed with pride. No one had ever praised him before.

"Now," Alex said. "I want you all to repeat after me: 'We're Rovers. We're winners. We're the best.'"

It took a few tries. Words like "winners" and "the best" were difficult to say. After a lot of laughter, they managed it.

In the end they were chanting it all around the park. "We're Rovers, we're winners, we're the best!"

"Good," Alex said. "We've made a start, but there's still a lot to work on. Be back here for practice tomorrow night."

Someone else had been watching the Rovers' practice session.

As the voices faded away, two figures crawled out from the bushes.

"Ahh! My leg is asleep!" Miles Elliot said, jumping up and down.

"Never mind your leg, who was that in the jogging suit?" Sean Slacker demanded.

"I don't know. Maybe it was Taylor's mom or something," Miles said.

"Don't be stupid!"

"Anyway, what are you worried about? We'll still clobber them on Saturday. You saw them. It took them ten corners before they got one in the goal."

"Who said I was worried?" Slacker said. "We'd beat them if they had a ten-goal advantage. Still… we don't want to take any chances, do we?"

"What do you mean?"

"Well, there's no way I'm going to let Taylor win our bet, so I bought something just to make sure."

Slacker brought a small box out of his pocket and showed it to Miles.

Miles read the writing on the label and grinned horribly.

"Itching powder. Does it work?"

Slacker nodded. "Agony – the strongest stuff in the store. It makes your eyes water and you can't stop scratching."

"Who should get it first?" Miles asked.

"I think it might help their goalie, don't you?" Slacker bared his pointed teeth in a smile of pure pleasure.

7

A Horrible Itch

As the big game drew closer, Kevin got more and more nervous. It seemed that every single person in Grimley knew about the Rovers and their record-breaking game.

Slacker had made sure that the news was all around the school. The newspaper story had done the rest. The Rovers' fame had spread far and wide. Kevin even had a phone call from a local TV producer who wanted to bring a camera crew to the match.

Alex had done her best. She had them out practicing after school every day.

By the end of ten practice sessions, there were signs they were getting better. Scuba, in particular, had started to save shots instead of diving aimlessly. For the first time they were passing the ball to each other.

Even Baby Joe had stopped trying to beat the whole team on his own.

Still, Kevin knew it wasn't enough. If they were playing someone else they might have had a slim chance, but not the Dixon Deli Dynamos. The Dynamos hadn't lost a game all season. Beating the Rovers would make them the league champions.

What's more, Kevin had seen Sean Slacker play. Even he had to admit that Slacker was the best player he knew.

No, the Rovers would need a miracle to avoid defeat.

Kevin couldn't even bring himself to think about the bet and the humiliation that was in store for him. He could almost taste the dirt on Slacker's cleats. It was going to be the worst day of his whole life.

On Saturday morning Scuba's dad drove his van into the parking lot. The Reject Rovers stared out of the windows in horror.

"Good gravy!" Mr. Horowitz said. "Look at these crowds. There must be a really big game today."

"There is, Dad," Scuba said miserably. "They've all come to see us lose."

"Oh, no! There's Amanda Ross from our class," Kevin said, ducking down behind a seat. Grinning faces pressed up against the van windows.

"Gonna lose! Gonna lose! Gonna lose!" they chanted.

The Rovers pushed their way through the jeering crowds to the locker rooms.

They were just unpacking their uniforms when there was a knock on the door. Sean Slacker came in.

"What do you want, Slacker? Your locker room's next door," Kevin said.

"You're not being a very good sport, Taylor. I just came to wish you good luck," Slacker protested.

"You just did. Now good-bye," Kevin said.

But Slacker insisted on going around to each Rover, one by one. He shook their hands and said he hoped they'd play well.

What was going on? As Kevin laced up his cleats, he wondered what his enemy was up to.

"Hey, what are you doing with my gloves?" Scuba said suddenly.

Slacker turned around. "Nothing! I was just taking a look," he said innocently.

He handed the red goalie's gloves back to Scuba. "Nice gloves," he said. "I bet you're just *itching* to get in the goal. Ha ha!"

Scuba looked at him as if he had a screw loose. Slacker paused at the door. "Well, good luck again, Rejects. You'll need it. Especially you, Taylor. My poor shoes are going to get extremely muddy today."

He stuck out his tongue and left.

Kevin turned his face to the wall. He felt like he was going to be seriously sick. Scuba and Alex were the only ones he'd told about the bet, but all the others had heard about it from Slacker.

Five minutes later there was a second knock on the door. This time they all shouted, "Get lost, Slacker!"

"It's me," said Alex. "Are you all changed? I thought we'd have a team talk."

Looking around the locker room, Alex could see how nervous they all were. The Rovers were used to playing in front of two or three people (and one of them was always reading the newspaper). Today there was a big crowd waiting for them. Everyone from school had come to see them lose.

Kevin was already panicking and Scuba couldn't stop scratching himself.

75

Alex did her best to calm their nerves.

"Forget the crowd," she said. "Forget how good the other side is. All you have to think about is yourselves. Today is your chance to shock them all. Show them that the Rovers are a soccer team, not a big joke. I know you can do it. I've seen you in practice. Let's hear you say it again: 'We're the Rovers. We're winners. We're the best!'"

They repeated their coach, as loud as they could, three times. Then they ran as fast as they could out on the field.

A huge cheer went up. Looking around, Kevin saw there were crowds on every side of the field. Even his mom and sister – who hated soccer – had come. He saw Steve Ryan from *The Grimley Gazette*. There was the TV crew behind their goal.

Kevin tried to calm his nerves by taking practice shots at Scuba.

Poor Scuba was in even worse shape. He kept tearing off his gloves to scratch at his hands.

"What's up?" Kevin asked.

"I don't know. It's my hands. They feel like they're on fire."

At the other end of the field, Sean Slacker and Miles Elliot were watching.

"It's working," Miles laughed. "Look, he's scratching himself like a dog."

"I'm not surprised," Slacker said. "I gave him the whole can. Half in each glove." He paused to thump a ball into the corner of the net. "The game's in the bag," he said.

A minute later they were lining up for the kickoff.

This is it, thought Kevin with the ball at his feet. The crowds of people were hushed.

"Come on, Dynamos!" someone called.

"Come on, clodhoppers!" someone else shouted.

There were roars of laughter.

The referee blew his whistle.

Kevin passed to Dancing Pete. Dancing Pete knocked it to Stringbean. Stringbean passed to Baby Joe out on the wing.

He beat two players, got to the line, and crossed, the way Alex had showed him. The Dynamos' goalie leaped and caught it, but the crowd had stopped laughing. They weren't expecting the Rovers to go on the attack. They had come to see them buried under an avalanche of goals.

For the first twenty minutes, the Rovers held their own. They got ten players back to defend. They ran hard. They passed the ball so well that the Dynamos had to work to get it back. They were playing well – apart from their goalie, who was acting more and more bizarre.

Scuba couldn't hold still. One minute his gloves were on, then they were off again. He danced around his goal as if ants were invading his uniform. Then disaster struck.

Sean Slacker got the ball just outside the penalty area. He looked up and saw Scuba bending down to pick up his gloves. Slacker let fly a stinging shot. It whistled over Scuba's head and into the top corner of the goal.

The crowd cheered and laughed. This was
what they'd come to see – the Rejects playing
like clowns.

"What are you doing?" Kevin hissed as he
took the ball from Scuba.

"I can't help it," Scuba groaned miserably.
"My hands are itching like crazy. I think it's
these gloves."

Kevin carried the ball back to kickoff.

"That's it," Dancing Pete told him
gloomily. "We'll never get back in the game
now. We're going to get slaughtered."

The goal had knocked the confidence out of the Rovers. They soon lost the ball. The Dynamos won a corner kick. It came over in the air and Scuba jumped to meet it. The ball floated straight into his waiting gloves. Then he fumbled it. Sean Slacker was on hand to slam it gleefully into the roof of the net.

2–0, Dynamos.

Scuba wished he could dig himself a deep hole. He imagined the goal being replayed in slow motion on the local TV news that night.

The Rovers had let in two goals in two minutes. They were starting to look like their old selves.

For the rest of the half they kicked the ball anywhere to clear it. The Dynamos hit the post and then the crossbar.

The Rovers rode their luck and were relieved to hear the half-time whistle.

Alex called all of them together to the center circle.

"What happened? You were playing so well. Then you went to pieces!"

"It's Scuba," Kevin said. "We'd still be in the game if it weren't for him. Now they're all over us." The others nodded in agreement.

Scuba stood there in misery, scratching at his wrists. "I can't help it!" he moaned. "Look at my hands, they're practically purple! Someone put something in my gloves." He showed them the orange dust caked inside.

Kevin had seen something like it in a joke shop. "It's itching powder!" he said. "It must have been Slacker, the dirty cheat! He was messing with Scuba's gloves when he came into our locker room. Wait till I get him!"

Alex had to hold Kevin back.

"It's no good starting a fight," she said. "You'll just get yourself kicked out. The only way to deal with cheats is to beat them at their own game. Go out there and get back in the match. Scuba, you can't play goalie with hands like that. You need to swap with Stringbean."

"What, me? Play goalie?" Stringbean stared at Alex.

"You told me that you were an excellent basketball player."

"Yes, but that's different."

"You'll be fine. Just use those long arms of yours. Now, the game's not over yet. You're only two goals down. Let's show Sean Slacker he isn't going to get away with this."

Kevin nodded. He glanced at Scuba, who was busy turning his gloves inside out.

"What are you doing now?"

"I've got an idea. Alex is right. You've got to beat cheats at their own game."

"What are you talking about, Scuba?"

"There's still plenty of powder in these gloves." He put them on inside out. "I'll be back in a minute," he said, and trotted over toward the Dynamos.

Kevin shook his head. Scuba had finally flipped. He watched him go up to Sean Slacker and slap him hard on the back of the neck.

"You're playing really well, Sean. Great goal!" Scuba said.

Slacker glared at him scornfully. "I've only just started. We're going to crush you losers this half!"

Scuba gave him a friendly wave. Then he went around to the rest of the Dynamos team, slapping and rubbing them on the back to congratulate them.

"What was that all about?" Kevin asked when Scuba trotted back.

"You'll see. I was just giving them a hand!" Scuba took up his position in defense.

The game restarted. The Dynamos went on the attack, looking for more easy goals.

Slacker took a pass with his back to the goal. Skillfully, he turned past Dangerous and kicked the ball between Scuba's legs. Slacker now had the goal at his mercy. There was only Stringbean to beat. Then, just as he was about to shoot, he started clawing at his neck.

"Yahhh! It stings!" Slacker hopped around as if he'd been bitten by a viper. Meanwhile, Scuba calmly took the ball away from him.

"Poor you – itching powder really is awful stuff," he said, shaking his head.

The Rovers took the ball upfield. The Dynamos tried to get it back, but now strange things were happening all over the field. The Dynamos were pulling off their shirts and scratching furiously at their backs.

The ball came to Kevin – he passed it to Baby Joe. The Dynamos player came out, then had to pause to scratch his neck. Baby Joe dribbled around him and scored; 2–1.

The crowd cheered and the Rovers celebrated their first goal in fifteen games.

Scuba gave Kevin a thumbs-up with the gloves. "Told you I'd given them a hand."

"Come on, Rovers, time for a second goal!" Alex shouted, jumping up and down with excitement. "You can do it!"

The Dixon Deli Dynamos were falling apart. The itching powder was affecting half their team. The other half of the players were keeping well away from Scuba.

Kevin went down the outside and passed inside to Scuba. Scuba advanced to the edge of the penalty area. Three Dynamo defenders blocked his path to the goal – but none of them wanted to risk a block. They seemed to be hypnotized by Scuba's deadly powdered gloves. While they hesitated, Scuba pushed the ball past them and tried a shot.

It scudded along the ground, hit a bump in front of the diving keeper, and bounced over him into the goal. Miraculously, the Rovers were tied.

As the Dynamos kicked off, Kevin could see the wonder on his teammates' faces. They thought they'd done it, that their losing streak was over. Kevin knew that for him, it wasn't enough. They had to win or he would still lose his bet with Slacker.

The thought of licking dirt from Slacker's cleats in front of everyone was too much to bear. He'd rather lie down in a tubful of maggots.

There were only fifteen minutes left. The Rovers needed one more goal, but their old failings started to show. Dancing Pete shot over the bar from five yards out and Kevin blew an easy chance by waiting too long.

The effect of the itching powder was starting to wear off. Sean Slacker looked dangerous at the other end. He would have scored twice if Stringbean's long arms and legs hadn't gotten in the way.

It was a nail-biting finish, with the crowd urging both sides forward to score.

Kevin chased the ball all over the field in desperation. As the final minutes ticked away, the Rovers won a corner kick.

Just as they'd practiced in training, Dancing Pete crossed and Kevin jumped to head it. He was going to score, until someone shoved him and he went sprawling.

"Tough luck, Taylor!" Slacker grinned, standing over him. Slacker's grin melted away when the referee's whistle blew. He'd seen the push and awarded the Rovers a penalty kick.

There was one problem. No one wanted to take it. The Rovers remembered too well their pictures in *The Grimley Gazette*. When Kevin offered them the ball they all shook their heads.

"Why don't you take it?" Scuba suggested.

"Me? Why me?" Kevin asked.

"You're the captain. It's your job."

"You guys, I'll panic. I'll probably miss... In fact, I know I will."

The referee impatiently blew his whistle again. They had to decide.

"Come on, Kevin!" Scuba said.

Kevin placed the ball on the spot. So it all came down to this. One shot. Just him and the goalie. If he missed they would all blame him – Kevin "Panic" Taylor – but not as much as he would blame himself.

He glanced up at the faces crowding behind the goal for a better view. There were his mom and sister, his classmates from school, and the TV camera zooming in on him. All were waiting for him to miss.

He felt the panic rising from somewhere in his stomach. He couldn't look at the goal. It would be shrinking smaller and smaller.

He tried to concentrate on the ball. If he could just kick it in the right direction so that he didn't look totally stupid...

Just as he was about to start his approach, a sneering voice said, "Whoops! Missed again, Kevin!"

Without looking, Kevin knew the voice was Slacker's. He felt a rush of fury.

He ran at the ball and thumped it with all his might. It went high and to his left.

The Dynamos' goalie flung himself and got one hand on it. For an awful moment, Kevin thought the goalie had saved it. Then the power of the shot took it past his fingertips and into the net.

There was a moment of stunned silence all around the field. Then the noise erupted.

Kevin was buried under a pile of players jumping on top of him. Alex was hugging everyone in the crowd, people she'd never met. Sean Slacker was chasing his own goalie around the field.

When the game finally restarted, it only lasted a minute. The referee blew his whistle. The Rovers had won. It was unbelievable.

They had beaten the Dixon Deli Dynamos. They wouldn't be claiming a place in the record books. They weren't The Worst Team in History. As Alex said later, "Even a professional team would have been proud of that performance."

Kevin was mobbed by friends from school. They all said that they knew the Rovers could do it all along.

The TV people were clamoring for an interview with him.

"Kevin, that was a shocking outcome," the reporter said. "How do you explain the difference in your team today?"

"Teamwork," Kevin said. "Thanks to our new coach, Alex, we've been improving all the time. The best is yet to come," he added with a grin.

"Did you always believe you could do it?"

"Of course," Kevin said. "In fact I had a bet on the outcome with someone. It revolved around cleaning a certain pair of cleats."

Kevin took off one of his shoes and held it up. It was caked in oozing brown mud.

"Has anyone seen Sean Slacker? I've got something for him."

Hiding in the middle of the crowd, Sean Slacker gulped. He tried to wriggle his way out, keeping his head down. Scuba was watching and grabbed him by the arm.

"Come on, Slacker," he said. "The cameras are waiting for you. Now it's your turn to make history."

About the Author

The idea for this story started with an article I came across in a newspaper. It was about an utterly terrible men's soccer team that had lost a record number of games in a row. It started me thinking what it would be like to play for the worst team in the world. The Reject Rovers are a little like some of the teams I played for when I was in school – so bad they can only get better!

Alan MacDonald